Just Be.

A COLLECTION OF POETRY

BY: HANNAH BEVIS & STORM LOVER

8TH & ATLAS PUBLISHING

8TH & ATLAS PUBLISHING

8th & Atlas Publishing
911 Walnut Street
Winston-Salem, NC 27101

www.8thandatlaspublishing.com

This book was ethically and responsibly
manufactured by Lightning Source.

Cover design and art by Victoria Haider

print ISBN: 978-1-7377181-4-7
ebook ISBN: 978-1-7377181-5-4

For the person that lives inside of all of us,
screaming to let them out. - SL

For the truth that you hold deep inside yourself
- listen to them. - HB

FROM HANNAH:

Writing a book takes a lot of time and effort, and there are many people in my life that I leaned on during that process. Endless thanks to:

My parents, for loving and supporting me in all of my endeavors, and especially my mom, for instilling a love of reading in me at a young age. I'd say that I'm sorry for all the nights I read at the dinner table...but I'm not.

My sister, Emma, for being a bright light in my life and one of my very best friends. I loved reading to you growing up, even if you fell asleep during some of it, and I couldn't ask for a better sibling to go through life with.

My unexpected but much beloved writing friends, Sara and Ali - I am continually delighted that we found each other at that poker table in Boston. You two have been wonderful friends and supporters in my writing endeavors, whether it was this book or some of my many other works in progress. Thank you both.

Meganna, my rock, my best friend, my whole heart, I am eternally grateful for you and all of the laughs and tears and wonderful times we have shared. Thank you for always being there for me.

Rebecca, Isa, and Audrey, my Haunted Liberators, for reminding me how wonderful it is to create something new, and for being some of my very dearest loves. To Rebecca, especially - thank you for making a home with me over the last couple of years. I am sorry for all of my incessant singing and whistling, but probably not sorry enough to stop (I'll do my best).

My friends that are too numerous to count - Angie, Molly, Emily D., Zoë, Alyx, Hia, Emily N., Sasky, and so many many others - you know who you are - thank you for making me laugh and feel loved. I love you all dearly.

And last, but certainly not least, this book would not exist without Storm, and I am eternally grateful for her. It was Storm who encouraged me to start writing poetry again, Storm who kept us on task, Storm who inspired me to give as much as I could to this project. I love you so, so, so much, and I am still so stunned that we were able to pull this off. You are the wind beneath my wings, and I hope we can keep flying together for a long, long time.

FROM STORM:

Bradley, for your bravery and gifting me stories I will cherish forever.

My love, Ashton, for treating this project like a carefully curated reality instead of just a fleeting dream since day one. You are my biggest supporter and the deepest love I've ever known.

My dad, for loving me through it all and getting me through the dark dark days so that I could breathe life into my writing.

Mr. Niezgoda, my high school poetry teacher. Thank you for teaching me the fundamentals that got me to where I am today. You were the first to ever read any of my poetry and you never wrote in red ink on my papers. I consider you my first fan, unbeknownst to you.

Kayleigh, DJ, Hannah, Luke, Emily, Narayan, Mona, Mark, Katie, Landon, Graham, Juan, Emma, Dane, Lake, Ang, Joey, and all the moms who've taken me in as their own, thank you for cheering me on through the years. You all are the reason I believe in myself.

And Vegas, for all of the deep conversations late into the night that always sparked my creativity. I think about you often and still wish I'd made your galaxy of words into a book full of poetry – even though I know you'd hate it. Thank you for loving my poetry.

ACKNOWLEDGMENTS:

Nicolette, for being the first person to read through this fully and offer thoughtful feedback.

Christina, Michael, & Brent at our amazing publisher who believed in our work and guided us to the finish line.

Our graphic designer, Victoria, for the heart she put into the illustrations and cover of this book. She's been on this ride with us since the beginning and was able to fully encompass our being through her artwork.

Dr. Seuss, Ocean Vuong, Catherine Kaufman, John-William Affourtit, Andrea Gibson, Sierra DeMulder, and Nikita Gill, for your creative expertise and inspiration.

All our book club babes - a blessing to each and every one of you for providing us with a constant, calm place to think, grow, learn, and laugh. To our LOTR crew - Ya hoi!

Angela and Robin for creating that magical space in Vermont where we got to share some of our poetry for the first time.

TABLE OF CONTENTS

In her beginning,
there were princess dresses and toy cars,
stuffed animals and scraped knees,
a sand table out back
and a sister to cradle.
There was time, and there was love,
and there she was,
living in it.

In my beginning,
there were Barbies in the wastebasket,
backyard adventures and LEGO pieces,
a baby blanket named Cassie
and insects in both hands.
There was time, and there was love,
and there I was,
living in it.

In our beginning,
there were thrift store clothes and first cars,
bonfires and yearbook pages,
homework that didn't matter
and races to be run.
Time was ticking, and life was scary,
and she met me,
surviving in it.

Somewhere in the middle
of the open and the close,

stands the two of us,
tethered together.
Though we do not know the way,
we do know this -
in the beginning, there was you, and there was me,
and in the now,
there is us.
For now,
that is enough.

- hb & sl

The Things We
Hold Inside

Every April,
my body decides it isn't safe anymore,
that existing hurts too much.

The changing of the season reminds her
how everything died in October.
That kind of loss is too much to hold;

"We do this every year," she says.
"Don't you ever get tired?"

The yes I hold in my throat is buried so deep,
I didn't think it could ever rise up from its tomb.
The weight is too much for one person (one body) to bear,
and though we try to bear it together,
it often feels more like a fight.

But we do have something else in common:
we're both looking for answers.
We've both spent so many wicked nights
crying, pleading to a universe that can't hear us
asking why life is worth living
when it feels like a struggle to even stay afloat.

It finally whispers back
life is everything -
the heavy and the light and the dark
and the sad and the joy
and the thousands of overcast days in between.

It is hard, and that's okay,
and you feel the hurt,
and that's okay too,
and you will feel,
and that's more than okay,
it's a goddamn miracle.

Growing is the hardest thing you'll ever do.

- hb

i'm sitting on the edge of a marina
watching the waves go by
my cold fingers attached
to this can of worms
that i haven't opened yet
because i don't want to
its outside still
shiny, yet
its insides lay
slimy, wet

i'm mad mad
if you use the same word twice
it gives it more power
i'm not just mad
i'm *mad* mad
always mad
sometimes sad

this little boy came up to me
he said he wanted to see
see what's in there
i told him there was no need
i don't even have a pole
they won't be good for anything
he begged me to open it anyway
began to cry when i told him no
threw a tantrum when it stayed closed

i could feel him banging his fists
on the inside walls of my heart
i didn't ask for this

"i want out!" he screamed
"i want to see what you see"
"i want to be out there with you"

i tell him i don't need him
that he's supposed to grow up

"you haven't let me," he cooed
"you locked me up,
made me stay down here,
away
from
you"

i'm *mad* mad
i have a little boy inside me
pushing his temper on me
he wants what i see
but i just want to be
left sad and all alone
with no one but me

- sl

Google Search History:
(After Caroline Kaufman)

burnout symptoms
how to know if youre burnt out
how to recover from burnout
am I addicted to my phone
what is codependency
what is religious trauma syndrome
how to know if you have cptsd

how to ask somebody out
how do you know if youre gay
how do you know if youre bi
how do you know if youre asexual
lgbtqia+ book recs

what is this stuff coming out of my vagina
define discharge
im nauseous on my period
how to relieve cramps
is it bad to masturbate
whats in a tampon
how to insert a tampon
define hymen
what is a vulva
will sex hurt
am i going to bleed my first time
how do you get pregnant

8

can you get pregnant without having sex
are some bodies not built for opposite sex sex
how to tell if youre pregnant

back pain
chest pain
heart palpitations
my heart wont stop racing
i cant sleep
i cant eat
do you ever stop having a period
how to know if you have breast cancer
how to know if you have ms
how to know if you have ocd
how to know if you have anxiety
i sleep too much
how to know if you have depression

how to make it all stop

- hb & sl

Guilt drags behind you, heavy and worn,
trips you up on the wooden floor.
You never used to notice it before,
now it follows you everywhere
a shadow so heavy
it wears down the soles of your shoes.

You gather it up gently,
carry it inside,
use it to cover that which you will not speak of,
tuck it carefully in a corner
deep and dark and secret.

Maybe ignoring it will make it easier to bear,
will make it disappear,
leaving no evidence behind
that it was ever even there.

You know that's not how this story ends,
but it's comforting to think that it could be.
You wrap yourself in this half-baked hope,
a warm blanket for when the weight feels like too much,
when the loathing gets too big,
threatens to swallow everything up

every shimmering summer day
and all your glow-in-the-dark laughter,
the velvet smooth fabric that carpets your heart,
the delicate chandeliers that whistle in the breeze,

all of your chocolate-filled greetings and flickering farewells,
each and every one of your decadent desires.

You carry them all to the curb
shining brightly in the rain.

It's not that you *want* to get rid of them.
You just don't think you deserve them anymore.

Maybe finding your truth means starting from scratch.

(Maybe if you say this to yourself enough, you'll start to believe it)

You lock the door behind you,
pull down the shutters over your eyelids,
tug your blanket around your shoulders,
raise your chin high as you can,
and wait.

For what, you still don't know.

- *hb*

This is your captain speaking,
before we take off
I'd like to remind you of a few things:
please keep your seatbelt securely fastened at all times...

Your heart's racing so fast
it deserves a gold medal
only winning doesn't feel like this,
white-hot flashes
of blinding panic.
Safety was a finish line
you passed miles ago.

You can find emergency exits
at the front and rear of the plane, as well as
two on each wing of the plane...

Should've just given me a parachute,
I'll find my own way off this lifeless tube.
Every exit is an emergency exit
if you try hard enough.
Anxiety doesn't follow instructions,
just flings you out the nearest window
and hopes you survive the fall.

Oxygen masks will fall in front of you,
please secure your own mask
before helping the person next to you...

I'm so used to gasping for air
I've forgotten how it feels
to take a deep breath,
too busy saving everyone around me
to notice that I'm the one who needed rescuing.
Now I don't have enough air
to ask for help.

Please turn off all your electronic devices
and place your seat in the full and upright position
until we have reached our cruising altitude...

There's a five-alarm fire raging in my body,
can't believe no one else can smell the smoke.
It's been ringing for two years now,
I keep hoping the battery will die,
but it runs on fear, and pain, and me,
it'll never turn off.

Please sit back, relax, and enjoy your flight.

- hb

"To the girl with a bubblegum smile and a dried up spine,
for the boy who found his happiness in a pill capsule,
for the long lost souls
who pinned their lives on the hope that better days beckon,
reached out for the light at the end of the tunnel
and got burned so badly
they could never recover."

"If only they had just tried harder:
drank more orange juice,
eaten more kale,
started a gratitude journal,
adjusted their attitude,
been more optimistic.
Don't you think that would have helped?"

The secret of the dark is its subtlety,
it doesn't come all at once, but in waves:
You begin to think it's normal:
the numbness that inserts itself into everything
the pile of clothes never washed
the kitchen sink stacked so high with dishes
that day by day become mountains.
You fear for the avalanche that will one day bury you,
complete the grave you've started digging yourself.

But digging your own grave requires effort,
something you haven't mustered up in months.

"Everyone here knows
how important exercise is,
it could have solved all their problems.
Why not try a jump rope–"

To immobilize you, not liberate you

"Take up lifting, buy some weights–"

You have plenty of those, they're just dragging you down

"Go for a walk, or a bike ride, or a run–"

*You've been running for so long, your soles are slapping
the pavement behind you*

"Maybe then you could have taken control of your life
started from scratch,
put all the pieces back together
don't you think if you had only just tried,
you would have gotten better?"

You can't even unearth the energy for a response

"Such a pity."

- hb

It wasn't forgiveness
as much as it was resentment getting too hard to carry.
It was for me, not for you.

Everything I tell you now feels so much heavier.
Underneath every new conversation
lies the weight still glittering under the surface.

It's not visible unless I'm crying,
my eyes, too glassy and bright to put up a shield,
can't hide the glint in them.

You think it's just innocence
but I know it's a spark
ready to burn down every single bridge in my line of sight.

I would burn the whole world down just to keep this promise to
myself: forgiveness does not mean forgetting.

Fighting isn't a sin when you threw the first punch.
I am not ready to hang up my boxing gloves quite yet,
I'm just learning when to pull my punches
instead of going for the knockout every time.

The only flowers growing in my garden are forget-me-nots,
to remind us both
that my fire isn't ever too far away.

Consider this your final warning.

- hb

Your whole childhood
from age three
to the end of seventeen
things happen to you.
mold you,
grab hold of you,
Sit You Up
and Fuck You Over.

Your whole adulthood
from age eighteen
to the end
you spend
undoing the things
once done.
Taking them out
and dumping them in
the trash bin.

- sl

Wish I could catch butterflies
the same way my body snatches my words from me;
lines them up on the shelves in my heart
screws the lids on too tight
so you don't hear the screaming.
There are no words for this
even if I still had any to say,
none of them would be enough.

When people tell you to ask for help
they don't realize that's a two-way street,
that me asking for help
is as simple as me existing,
that me getting out of bed was asking for help,
and brushing my teeth and taking a shower and walking outside,
for fuck's sake
it would have been so much easier to give up,
stay home,
smother myself in my blankets
close my eyes
and wait for my words to come back.

This is what I wish you would say to me:

I'll help you catch your breath,
in my homemade safety net;
I wove it myself
on all the nights I couldn't sleep, either.

I cannot put out all the fires that rip through your body,
but I will help you cry them out,
kiss your mouth open to let the steam fog up the glass,
steep the heat in water still hot from the kettle,
tip the teacup softly to your lips.

I will lie here with you,
until your legs feel less heavy,
and your heart feels more ready,

and even if you are never ready,
I will still be here with you.

- hb

Things That Go Missing Are Not Things Still Existing

when we talk
i walk away more lonely
than when we began

- *sl*

I can feel rainbow headed fabric pins puncturing
the cavities of my heart
a gentle, slow-consuming pain.
Like the growing of a tiny seed
this long-rooted pain supersedes
my brain's once loving reign.
As my heart becomes covered in multicolored beads
it looks just like a children's ball pit in the midst of COVID-19
completely empty, not a kid in sight, not even a teen.

I feel so much loneliness and rejection
a complete lack of affection.
I'm completely worthless to them:
my own family, both of my parents.
Why couldn't I be what they wanted?
Why didn't they want me?
I was always just too short of perfection
left with this awful disconnection.

I feel angry and sad and completely wasted on
cheap vodka all at the same time.
Like the seafood stew, *chef's special*,
"Here is the oldest fish I'm legally allowed to sell you,
diced and cooked all together."

It comes on so unexpected
just like my period, except
instead of once a month
it comes and goes, just whenever.
Doesn't matter if I'm *spoken for,*
speaking with, or sleeping with
all I feel like is sleeping in.

Because I'm so tired,
endlessly exhausted
like a new mother laying there after fourteen hours of labor,
but without the gift of a new baby
instead just another reminder that I was the child
she didn't want.

And it doesn't matter how many sad poems I write
it won't change a fucking thing.
I'll still be some kind of Peter Pan,
leading Lost Boys to Nowhere instead of Neverland.

- *sl*

The secret is this:
you can get used to drowning,
forget the days before
you lived with water in your lungs,
when every breath wasn't a gasp for air,
forget what it felt like to just live your life,
and not fight for it.

The end of your life doesn't come all at once,
it happens slowly,
a drip, drip, dripping
so quiet
you don't even notice
until you're already knee-deep and sinking fast.

Bury it so deep in your chest
that nobody can find it,
not even you.

Things that go missing
aren't things still existing.

I'll keep the lock,
and swallow the key.
Good luck opening me up.

- *hb*

You spend your whole life somewhere
only to leave, and to come back
and to find that nobody remembers you.

You're an opaque ghost filled with
nothing but vague memories.

Roaming streets that now haunt you,
echoing words from forgotten pasts.

Whispering televised histories,
erasing you from all of them.

You don't exist,
you don't belong here,
you never did.

- *sl*

sometimes
when i don't know what to say
or who to call
or where to stay
i wrap my arms around
my denim legs
and tuck my head
in between rusted days

- sl

Loneliness is nocturnal,
feels bigger in the nighttime,
feels wider on a Friday
with a weekend on the horizon
and no one else to spend it with.

Numb my insides with the cheapest liquor I can find,
block out the world with my broken headphones.
They're falling apart,
just like everything else I own,
but they still work most of the time
so I tell myself I can still get by;
I've held on to this lie
since April.

I sway in the glimmering nothing,
eyes shut tight,
gifting myself the only darkness
I have any control over.

This is how you fend off fear:
with a cheap bottle of wine,
a special playlist for the occasion,
burnt-out Christmas lights
and a far-flung hope
that maybe someday
you can bottle this feeling up
to knock it back on the nights
when the empty brings you to the brink
of the wide open nothing you call home.

- *hb*

Driving home alone
is not something I condone.
It's dark
& I don't ever want to get there
because once I park
it's this feeling I cannot bear;
this empty, lonely,
sad longing
for anyone but me.

But only at night
when the blackness creeps over me
& the moon's nowhere in sight,
only then
do I feel completely desolate.
My mind goes to all of the places
I've been hiding from it.
My heart feels less than running on low
and the rest of me sinks into more nothing
until I'm completely alone.

- sl

Nobody Said Healing Was Easy

Last year
I wrote a book
with a blank cover.
it didn't have a title,
it would never be published.
No chapters or sections
or preludes or introductions.
When you opened the first page
it simply began
and on the last page
it ended.

We were kind of like that.
We met one random day in the spring
my car got towed at your apartment complex.
You took me to Coldstone to make it better
then drove me to the tow impound
and suddenly we were two, bound.

You drove me from one job to the other,
kept your eyes on the road when I changed uniforms in your pas-
senger seat.
Brought me three kinds of eyeliner when I ran out
(how could you know which kind I liked?)
and cold coffee to keep me awake during my eighty hour work
week.

You taught me to add salt when I boil water,
that it's okay to love someone for who they are
and not who they're going to be,
that I could two-step in the middle of a forest
when nobody was watching me.

I learned so much from you, Best Friend.
At some point, I hope I was yours too.

I felt I really saw you, all of you.
I only hoped you saw me too.

But then one day we closed our cover.
We ended.
And we never finished the blank book
that we'd been writing together.
So I finished it.
Alone.

I felt like I had to;
I thought it might give me clues
to what happened to you
or give me closure
maybe bring us closer
the never ending saga of me and you.

I started cooking more spaghetti,
traced the salt-grain constellations floating in its water,
stopped wearing eyeliner and paid more attention to the
sharpness of my brow than the wings on my lids,
still can't look at a cold brew without seeing you,
fogging up the glass with your misplaced self-deprecation.

Writing the book alone made me sad too,
the same way it did to you,
except you weren't alone—
that you should have known.

But in the end I finished it, using only 6 words
6 words I have heard lots of times
but never all together
6 words I've written down a hundred times
but never believed

6 words I wished somebody would say to me
but never did
6 words that I want to say and mean
but never have
6 words that I want to gift to you.

Because I wish this for you and know it will come true:
"Everything's going to be all right"

Everything's going to be alright.
Everything is going to be alright

- sl

You will know it when you taste it -
bitter, like the truth,
hopeful, like the past, or the future, or maybe both.
It's hard to swallow, but you know you must.
Thrust it past your lips like the bubble gum pink syrup
you choked down when you were too small to protest.
Let it melt on your tongue,
drip down your throat
fill you with heat.

The thawing is slow, love,
because that's the way it has to be.
Bitter, but brave,
hopeful, but hard.

A tough pill to swallow, for certain,
but nobody ever said healing was easy.

- hb

To everyone I never asked
here is a list of everything,
and I mean *everything*
I've tried to keep my hopelessness at bay:

Praying to a God I stopped believing in,
believing in God again,
sleeping more, eating less,
drinking more,
caring less,
giving up,
trying again,
giving in,
sitting up,
trying again,
and again
and again and again andagainandagainandagainand

It is a practice,
a daily routine.
To blink back into existence
from a comforting and quiet dark.
Claw back into a world
that is so unforgiving,
harsh and loud,
a living more like a shattering of glass
where the shards follow you everywhere
nicking and shredding pieces of you constantly
reflecting back a life you no longer recognize.

I am Atlas, the whole world on my shoulders,
I am Icarus, too close to the sun,

I am every cliche of someone who fancied themself a god
before life beat them into submission.

The Herculean effort of living is still here
pounding steadily in my chest
flexes when I take a shower,
brush my teeth,
change for work,
leave the house.

Some days it takes every bit of power
to roll out of bed.
I attempt this feat anyways,
because there is often nothing else to do but what you can.

It was never about arriving at a destination -
the top of a mountain, the sun, the moon, the stars.

It is only ever the movement it takes to get there -
tying my shoes, shouldering my pack, fixing my eyes on the road
ahead.

Close your eyes, breathe deeply.
Take your first step a little easier,
knowing that behind you, there are thousands of others attempting
this dangerous, daring, spectacular feat with you

even if there is no one there to applaud but us.

- hb

You could bury my grief in good intentions;
set fire to it,
cast it away in the sea of all the tears I never shed
because my body wouldn't let me,
because if one single drop had found its way
past the dam that guards my heart
I would have drowned everyone in it, including myself,
which feels like a fair price to pay
as long as you'd get caught in the current, too.

You tell me so often how much it hurts,
that what we had was special,
that you miss it every day,
and that you are just waiting on me to grant you the forgiveness
you so desperately seek.

Can I wield forgiveness like a weapon?
It feels like that's what you're asking me:
to raise it high above my head
and slice up the past,
destroy it so utterly
that I wipe it from existence.
That is the only way
things will go back to "normal."

I have looked to forgiveness as a solution for so long
that I've forgotten to tend to my grief.
I miss you so much that my stomach aches
but you can't return what's been taken away.

Today I will love my grief back to life
because she will live with me forever.

Maybe once she's healthy again
we can try to bridge the gap between us
one last time.

- *hb*

You unfasten the buttons on your shirt
loosen the collar
alter the sides
tie the ends into a knot
cuff your sleeves
do everything you think you can do to change
but no matter what
you're still dressed in black scars and ugly shades
of red, white, and blue
with thirteen not-so-spangled stars.

The worst are those that figured out how to discard their shirts
tossed them in a back alley dumpster
can't even recall what they looked like
or if they had ever really worn them.
If we pretend it never happened
then racism doesn't exist.

Yet those who were taught it was the War of Northern Aggression
instead of the war of slavery neglection
still grow up to be just like the adults who wore
these clothes before them.
Not realizing they're repeating the same mistakes
not realizing they're moving on with higher stakes
that they just pulled another collared white shirt
over the head of another starry-eyed kid.

We've done such a bad job of stopping the cycle
plain and simple—we created white dismissal.
Now we have to sit and see if our children can figure out
just how *not* to recycle
undo the buttons on that same shirt

and stop this never ending succession
of viewer's discretion:
An Everlasting White Impression.

- sl

Twenty-Twenty

Ten years ago I was thirteen.

My big brother was a heroin addict.

My mom packed her suitcase and left us.

I found out I liked boys—and girls.

I had my first love, and second, and third.

I went to college. I dropped out of college. I went to beauty school.
I went back to college.

I moved south then north then east.

My brother got sober and married.

I was a janitor, a bike seller, a photographer, a forklift driver,
a science teacher, and now a barber.

I tell you all of this to tell you this:

Things change.

And the next ten years will be as unpredictable as the last.

- sl

You start forgetting
why life wasn't worth living;
a whole world lifted.

- *hb*

You Are Radiant
As You Are

September feels hopeful,
for the first time in a long time.
I feel the cold but don't shiver.

Last year I tried to become a butterfly,
pulled my blankets around me,
built a chrysalis,
hoped with every fiber of my being
that I would emerge as something different.

I couldn't, of course.
I stayed rooted exactly where I am.
Disappointed, I burrowed myself down into the dirt.
It's a sorry excuse for warmth,
but back then, it's all I had.

I learned,
eventually,
there's more than one way to change,
to grow,
to become.

I found out there are other ways to fly,
instead of waiting for wings
that were never my birthright;

Happiness feels different now.
I live with less abandon
and have welcomed home safety,
built a cocoon from contentment,
wrapped myself in hope
warmer than a hundred wool blankets.

I find peace in my own body,
breathe easy,
welcome myself home.

- hb

You do not have to be polished,
sitting pretty, staying pretty.
You do not have to be perfect,
prim or proper.

Your love is a wide open field,
a highway that never ends;
no borders could ever hold it,
and why would you want them to?

You are radiant as you are.

You have carried judgment so long, child,
held the knife to your own throat
and blamed others for holding you hostage.
Until you learn to forgive yourself
that sharp steel will never leave you.

Gift yourself permission to feel,
let your tears fall to the floor,
let them transform you.
You are weightless now -
let go.

- *hb*

wipe off my makeup
i don't need to be made up
self conscious break up

- sl

You push away your "nos"
to the back of your throat,
think maybe if you swallow them whole
you will finally be good enough.

You still think worth is measured
in percentage points;
think that going to church and volunteering gives you extra credit in
compassion, in kindness, in making a good first impression.
You get straight A's in being well-rounded
but flunk out of being human.

You learn to speak only when spoken to
(even though you don't feel like anyone can hear you)
You lower your voice, keep your eyes on the floor,
get top marks for fitting in,
but it still doesn't make you feel wanted.

There is no passing or failing at life,
only living it.

I wish I could tell you
that your wholeness is not measured by obedience,
your happiness not tied to your test grades,
that all of those trophies you win
will do nothing for your self esteem,
only collect dust in the corner of your heart.

Making yourself smaller
does not build yourself up,
just gives you less room to breathe on the bad days
and though you don't have many of them now,

they are coming,
and they will destroy you.

I am giving you permission now
to hurt, to scream,
to cry and kick and wail,
to feel your pain fully
instead of folding it neatly and tucking it away.

You've always been so messy, so scatterbrained and untidy.
Why is it that your righteous anger is the only thing that's always
kept locked away, always in its proper place, out of sight where
nobody can see it,
not even you?

I hold on to my past so hard
that I get blisters on my palms.
My five- and seven- and ten- and thirteen-year-old selves
can't keep my anger locked up anymore.
When it roars out of hiding,
filling every corner of my body,
burning whatever stands in the way,
I wish I could tell myself
that this is the most important moment of your life.

This fire is angry, yes, out of control, furious,
and it is also mine.
I will learn to love it,
to show the children that still live with me
that this hellacious, sinister, sizzling part of us
was never something to be ashamed of
in the first place.

All new beginnings smell like smoke.

- *hb*

49

Someday I'll love Storm
(After Ocean Vuong)

A lifetime spent running from her
I didn't want to be like her
I wanted to be called ordinary
I wanted to be normal.

So, she changed for me
moved states for me, built brains, gained weight,
threw out her comic books, cut off her curly locks–
all for me.
She put five new holes in her ears
filled as much skin as she could hide with ink
trying to conceal the one part of herself that was still there
lied about where she came from
tried to marry a not-so-family man
and
spent her whole life impersonating the enemy
the people she never wanted to be like
the ones who mocked her
who put out her light.

I never knew how to tell her
I didn't want this from her
and somehow that made me the enemy too.
Soon I became her and she became me
And together we let ourselves just be.

- sl

Someday I'll love Hannah
(After Ocean Vuong)

When you wake up tomorrow,
and no longer recognize
the person staring back at you in the mirror,
do not be afraid.

Scratch that;
allow yourself to feel afraid,
to let fear rip through you.
Give it entry,
pour it some tea,
tell it to leave its shoes by the door.

Feel it fully.

*The most beautiful part of your body
is where it's headed.*

Tell that to me in January,
when nothing about my body is beautiful.
It riots against me on the daily,
leaves the sink running for hours on end,
sets off the fire alarm,
tears books from the shelves,
drops them to the floor,
burns them to ashes,
and locks every exit with me still inside.

My stomach shuts down for weeks,
then months.

My memory starts to go.
I don't remember the days when everything didn't hurt.
My eyes won't stop leaking,
I go through a whole box of tissues
in one therapy session;
I walked the quarter mile to get to that appointment,
because I listened to the voice in my head that said
I would die if I got in the car.

It told me that a lot, those days
that I would die no matter what I did.
So I stopped doing everything.

Saving yourself isn't supposed to look like this.
But mine did.

The most beautiful part of your body
is that it always has your best interest at heart.
It might not always know how to tell you that,
but it knows it must tell you somehow.
So it kicks and screams,
bloodies and bruises itself,
does everything in its power to get your attention,
because it loves you so hard
it makes your teeth hurt,
your bones ache.
This love isn't soft or tender,
but strong,
powerful,
the kind of love that causes earthquakes,
that mends broken hearts,
that starts and finishes wars.

It is time to lay down your weapons.

The most beautiful part of your body
is that it loves you.

It whispers to you softly:
Time to return the favor.

- hb

Still Weird
Still Queer

i can't just say it
i have to display it
showcase it
face it
be okay with it
but this gay in me
is *so* not okay with me

- sl

It lived next to the screaming
to the slammed doors
never got a word in
too busy trying to climb past
the stony silences

After all this implicit violence
why do you think
I never let even a sliver of it
slip past my tightly sealed lips?

- *hb*

We were laying in a dark room
clothes on,
(thank god)
and you asked me about the craziest thing I'd ever done.

I don't even know how to answer you,
but I try to,
because the longer I talk,
the longer we don't have to kiss,
the less I have to worry about
when this unspoken expectation will swallow me up
and whether or not
it will spit me back out.

I've already closed my door to you;
tried too hard to be someone you want,
never once thinking
of what I needed,
never deemed myself enough to even pose the question.

And fuck me,
(but don't, please)
I don't even know how to write this poem,
don't know what words to use
to explain to you
what this feels like,

I'm building this cathedral
with blueprints that don't exist;
I'm standing there with two support beams,
and nothing to connect them with,
I don't have time to figure it out;

I have to return this bulldozer by midnight.

I want to scream,
and cry,
and just be held,
and loved,
but I don't know who can do it
don't know who will understand it,
who will understand me.
My whole life
has been one big misunderstanding
and now that's woven into the fabric of who I am.

The craziest thing I've ever done
is turn that evil in on myself,
and think that I could turn me good,
I mean turn me on,
I mean turn undone,
twist myself inside out,
into the opposite of who I was
into what you want me to be.

It is all I have ever wanted
but it is only now I'm realizing
that it was never meant to be.

It will take a lifetime to unlearn.

This, at least,
I can begin now.

- hb

For Bradley –

The first time I matched with a girl on Tinder
I remember thinking
oh god, what the fuck do I send her?
I agonized over it
and eventually decided nothing at all
was a better call
than to say something off the wall
she couldn't possibly be interested
I mean, what gay girl dates on Tinder?

But then one day I bumped into her
I was walking home from class,
did a turn and pass
stopped her right in her tracks

We both giggled, each of us knowing
who the other was,
each of us wondering why the other
never hit send after typing an easy
"H", "E", double hockey sticks, "O"
We both blushed, my face much more flushed
which is how she knew I wouldn't say no
to her invite out

This wonderful woman
so suave and devout
she made me feel so hot,
so smart and lovely throughout

The only tiff we ever spit:

who would take the lead, who would drive
who would pay
who was more virile, more mannish
more macho
she was so esse quam videri
because she was
and I only kind of was
our battles proved unnecessary

Nothing too grand about our story
I wasn't ready to accept the love
she was so ready to give me

We parted,
Our relationship preserved
as kind and lighthearted

She struggled with things
her own demons, and eating
and sobriety
all horribly torturous things

But then one day she set herself free
and she became he
like I said, (s)he was different from me

I thought if I had stayed with her
I would have stayed with him
and I think that there are more people this way
more that would be okay with this kind of gay
this kind of fluidity
that is if we weren't always worried about
others' validity

This girl I once knew
grew into the man who was always there
Wears the name "Bradley" as a gold medal
to celebrate the coming into himself

that I'm sure was the hardest thing he'd ever done

Bradley is much more happy
and truthfully
Bradley is who he always was
the funniest, the wittiest
the whole package deal

He is
the man

He is
trans

He is perfect
to a pan

- sl

You're pretty,
I know, what a pity.
Let's get back to the nitty gritty of this inner city.
I know you're a man and I'm more than a fan.
(I should have written this in crayon so you could see how childish
you're being)
Quit disagreeing, I'm guaranteeing.
Don't make me get political
enticing, dreamy, or irresistible–
either way you're my evening muse,
the pep in my shoes
the sugar to my tea
the honey to my bee.
Don't you see?
I'm giddy 'cus you're pretty.
It doesn't matter how I say it;
this fight is archaic
girl, boy, he, she
you're still the prettiest I see.

- sl

I am tired of viewing intimacy
as a straight line
with sex at the end
and everywhere in between
just mile markers
keeping the time.

How far did you get?
How fast did you go?
You ignore any detours and cul-de-sacs and winding, wistful side
roads,
but those are the streets that I try to make my home;
pounding pavement,
covering every square inch of them
but never actually arriving anywhere.

Just moving, keep moving,
don't put roots down for too long
or you'll get stuck
can't pull your feet back up
worried too much about where you'll head next
in a world where you never seem welcome.

It's exhausting, living like this.
Someone keeps stealing my stop signs at night,
fucking with my traffic lights so that it's always
yellow, yellow, yellow,
maybe, maybe, maybe,
an echo that never shuts off;
'no' doesn't last very long here.

It didn't used to be this way:

I could hold your hand and it would be sweet, not a promise,
braid your hair and it was a kindness, not a flirtation;
the butterflies in my stomach,
the warm light that nested deep in my chest,
the kind of smiles where you just can't help yourself,
that feeling of home
used to be enough, not just a stepping stone.
When did that change?

I leave the main roads alone;
they were never meant for me
I've made peace with that now.
Started making my way through the long-forgotten
back trails instead.
It's quieter here, and more open -
the kind of place where expectation
doesn't have to bloom into something else.

The kind of place you could build a life in.

- hb

i am pan
not the kind you hold and shake and flip to bake
but the kind nobody can quite understand

i'm not interested in muscles or collars
or chest hair or skin colors
nor do I require hourglass shapes
or for the carpet to match the drapes
so what if you're a he or she
a them or a hen
either/or works for me

i like a flustered grin
and a devilish personality
even if our sexuality
is a forbidden sin

i dig quick wit
a heart that doesn't quit
legit grit
and not giving a shit.

i want someone
full of freehanded sunshine
to pine for
who secretly likes how i publicize
that i think they're fine,
my kind of dime
and no matter what size
they should definitely be mine

i love souls not sexes

timeless aesthetics
seem as useless as WiFi
without a connection
i want a gentle intellectual
outward perfection
to an awkward pansexual
holds no inherent merit,
it's just some thing you inherit

maybe that makes me semi demi

if i peel off all your skin, what will be left?

that's what i see
that's what attracts me to you
like a firefly to a flashlight
i just want to touch your flame
see if you light me up inside,
shoot me up like a kite and calm my tide.
see if maybe you want someone
that loves you for
you
and if maybe
you can love me for me,
too

- sl

All The Watercolors That Paint Our Hearts

(After April Fleck)

you were my first love
my longest love
my see-other-people
but never get over it love

- *sl*

Vacancy
rooms available
nobody's home
that's the sign
hanging on my heart

I read yours:
Occupancy
unavailable
this isn't your home

monochrome memories
remind me I was blind and unkind
and so I'm forced to sit
outside your door
hands tied
wishing forever
I'd had the courage
to just knock

- sl

I'll never stop loving you
like a teenage girl
you always take me back
to those years
where everything was simpler
and love was trivial
but now it's so serial
and my heart beats
sound amplified
sitting next to you
warm bodied
without sweating
color me blushed
staring into you
wishing for nothing more
then to be held by you
and loved back too

- *sl*

I grew up surrounded by people promising me
that one day I would stumble through love's double doors
and be caught by a faceless someone
and that that would be the end of my story.

Cue the credits, cut the cake, take off your shoes, and dance
until you throw up the four glasses of wine you had at the open bar,
forget to write the thank-you notes,
cancel your honeymoon,
yell at your new Forever Someone
while wishing you didn't have to share your bed with them.

That love is a place, not a knowing,
a noun, not a verb,
a fantastic getaway destination
that you can't actually get away from.

Why have we condensed that passion so intensely,
watered her down,
made her more performative than feeling,
more of a checklist than a revealing
of your inner hopes, dreams, and desires
of how to build a wonderful life with someone you cherish,

and why don't we allow that someone to be you?

My fierce devotion holds me close,
tells me to not try to contain her,
does not want to be tied up in a bouquet
nested among the forget-me-nots and bleeding hearts,
simply waiting to wilt away in a vase.

She will find her own way,
she will find her own heart,
she will not be restrained.

This is love, this is home,
a wild and fierce becoming
that breathes as deeply as you or I
and lives on long after we pass through.

I hope you might meet her some day, too.

- *hb*

Part I

I feel like I could commit
I feel like I could vomit

- sl

Part II

Your venomous words fill my air
"It's not what you said, it's how you said it."
So many miles away and still not enough room to breathe,
did you ever really care?
I know, I'm throwing a fit.
You've seen my temperament.
Let's end this torturous affair
just because you can't fucking commit.
It's always you. you. you.
You're a counterfeit. So unfit. A hypocrite.
A power couple who couldn't power on together.
Like soured milk you left a bad taste in my mouth.
New phone, who dis? No, none of this.
Got a new phone number, kissed you goodbye—remember?
Sad I had to let your family go, but Cupid took back his arrow.

Here's the thing:
the part of me that hates you thinks you're a liar,
that this whole thing was a scandal.
But the rest of me that knows you
thinks you just don't know how to love,
or maybe you forgot how to.
You're stubborn and have no plans to change.
My, how the tables have turned.
I know you think I'm hurting you,
that I'm not playing fair.
Maybe you think I'm the one who doesn't care.
Too bad you'd be wrong.
I cared too much.
And now my heart's left with a tear.

- *sl*

I miss Vegas
walking down the strip with pockets jingling
you were such an intoxication
with your shiny slot machines
and giant versions of regular things

I miss Vegas
as I danced down the sleazy streets
you poured Jameson down my emptiness
stuck bandaids on me for temporary happiness
tried to trade away my self-destructive tendencies
with nothing but a jar full of blackened pennies

I miss Vegas
I wondered if we'd get married
by Elvis, with cheap plastic rings
if they'd call us Bonnie and Clyde
all we'd need was a getaway ride

I miss Vegas
but we all know how that story goes
or rather, abruptly ends
with bullets in their heads

you offered me the world
when all I could fill you with was silver coins and dollar bills
I know you didn't mind
your happiness wasn't everything
it was me you wanted smiling

but I was so powerless
against the scam surrounding us

I was washing filthy streets
with a brushless sweep
the people, I mean, the trash,
no, the trashy-people kept multiplying
pushed you out of this stronghold you were occupying
took over the only city you ever truly loved

and in the midst I fucked you up
couldn't love you the way you loved me
"You don't have to force yourself to say it,
I want you to mean it."
You said that once to me
and told me not to put your words into poems

but you also said if you couldn't, you wouldn't love me
you would erase me from your mind
but that you'd never be able to (me either).
That's an oxymoron though,
"If I could not, I would not Love you."
Well I would not, could not Love you Sam-I-Am
It is not, was not, what we had
You have not, will not ever know
just how my heart spoke so

no more get rich, fall in love quick
Land of Magnificent Things.
Just a Joker tossed from a game of golf
and a broken King of Hearts
weighed down by an old deck of cards.

- *sl*

I hate that I still care about you
I've never spent so much time worrying about someone
who I don't think worried about me
you lusted for me.
you were greedy with me.
you made me feel like an object
something to obtain,
gain,
another trophy for your dusty window pane
have you not wiped a hand through that dust?
can you still not see?
I loved you, I love you
without a single
standard
set.

You could be anything,
a sloth filled with wrath and gluttony
envying my everything.
Still I kept you under my wing.
Remember when you said
"If you meet somebody I'll just sort of fade away"
and I told you "No, no, how about you just go away,"
it hurt so bad that day
but in a new way
like
instead of breaking my heart
you made it realize you never really cared about it anyway.
Just you.
And your heart.

Greed. Lust. Wrath. Sloth. Gluttony. Envy.

You were all of these things to me,
but never pride. And maybe that's why
I saw everything in you,
but you never noticed
because you saw too much in me.
I couldn't be with you because you couldn't be with you.
I loved you exactly the way you wanted me to love you.
That's the part you got wrong.
I know because walking away from someone never hurt as much as
closing the door to you did.
You said you wanted me to be happy
but you never did sit and watch how happy I could be.

- *sl*

Today I learn
that sushi was made from rice
soaked in vinegar
simmering, fermenting, stewing
for hours, days, months.
Sounds like us, I think,
or rather, sounds like me.
Sushi comes from an older term,
one that means sour-tasting.
That explains why I haven't been able to get
the taste of metal out of my mouth
since last October.

I've tried to write this poem
for nearly a year now.
You may never see it,
but I still feel
as though I owe it to you.

Every time I speak to you,
I feel like it should start with an apology.
I'm sorry, how was your day?
I'm sorry, what's going on?
I'm sorry, you don't have to keep apologizing,
I know it's a habit of yours,
but please don't ask forgiveness for everything you say.
It should be me
begging for your pardon,
not you, never you.

I should know your order by heart now,
but I don't, so you tell me:

California roll, spicy tuna, miso soup.
I hand you my soy sauce,
you pour me some wine.
We spend a whole summer like this.

I couldn't tell you at what point things changed,
nor could I tell you how, exactly.
All I know is I wrapped everything up too tightly,
used soy paper to hold it all in,
thinking that if I just said nothing
maybe I could hold everything together.
But if you pressed me,
I don't think I could tell you what *everything* is,
only that it keeps me up late with a stomach ache.

We're driving home late one night,
the highway empty, save for the odd streetlight.
I tell you I don't know what I believe in anymore,
but that I do believe in love;

I've spent every day since asking what kind of love I'm talking
about.

I wish my sexuality didn't feel like an apology,
that loving this way wasn't so hard.
I'm sorry, I love you,
I'm sorry, I miss you,
I'm sorry, please go,
before I hurt you again.

I should know my own heart by now,
but I don't.
I'm just so sorry
that yours got caught in the cross-fire.

- hb

A Jacob's ladder romance
not two strings, but one loop.

My heart bangs against yours like a paddleball battleground.
Specks of sea mist twirl around your two-eyed merry-go-round.
You have me drowned in drunken feelings of things
I had forgotten I could feel.
I'm so drunk on your warmth. So whole with you.

I never *was* very good at feeling.

There's these soft, sexy lips on mine,
sloppy tongues entangling and wrestling the love out of each other.
I don't even care how your beard scratches the edges of my mouth
or that my hair is spread like feathers on a pillow,
that my foundation is being rubbed off by your freckled skin.
Soon you'll know that the complexion surrounding my open mouth
is more of a blush pink than a clean matte
and that my eyebrows aren't quite as angular
as I make them up to be.
And suddenly I can't remember why I had gowned myself with
these things in the first place.
Would you really not have noticed me without all these carefully
placed brush strokes?
Would it have stopped you from tipping the lip of your teapot into
my heart?
Watching as it fills me with steamed yearning.
Yearning for more of this unsolicited intoxication.
Knowing now that you like all the parts of me
I thought I had to hide.
Unkempt but well kept
My body was designed

Perfectly imperfect like a used candle
With wax cascading on all sides.

Why is it I'm not skittish around your affection?
Why do you make the soft dips in my cheeks pull the corners to my
lips so wide?

We were each other's selection
both having felt the connection.
You think I'm tidy, noticed my clean fingernails, saw my put-to-
getherness, commented on my effortlessness captured in my hair.

You see the things I want to see but have been told are not there.

Because of you
things are now under repair.
I'm disposing of all my bad hardware,
removing all the malware,
cleaning out the closet, clearing out the cabinets, and emptying the
toaster tray.

I'm taking my insides out, placing them on display.

There's finally *construction underway.*

- sl

You dropped a match down my throat
set fire to my desert heart,
left an eternal flame
like a soft and slow burning candle.

Listening to you sing
as you drench my lungs with gasoline
let it leak from my rib bones,
flick open your lighter,
smile while I can't breathe.

Till the fireworks go off
a thousand tiny explosions,
all in my chest.

That's how this love feels;
it hurts and it's real.

For weeks I've wished I could peel this love off
just like an old sunburn and watch it fall to the sand.

But last night I finally whispered to you just how I feel
three little words and a name attached to the front of them.

My heart nearly burst,
I felt just like a schoolgirl asking the teacher for help on a test—
like I shouldn't be doing it.
But if I didn't I might not pass,
if I didn't I might actually burst.

So I whispered them.

I ignored the teacher telling me to "speak up"
instead I rest in the silence-filled air
my back against you
your arms wrapped around me
snug on my skin
and nervously,
you whispered them back.

Your match hasn't stopped falling down my throat
adding more fuel to the fire, giving me heat stroke.

When you're around my cheeks burn bright
turn this desert Storm to fire with one lightning strike.

My sunburned skin now flaunts a sun-kissed tan.
I think I'll keep lying with you in this yellow sand.

- sl

I've been thinking lots about love lately.
You know the one -
it's in all the movies and TV
the only *real* love
we're ever permitted to see.

Love-love has lots of rules,
like how many times you can kiss in public
or how long you're allowed to hold hands
without making other people squirm.
You can cut that time in half if you're queer,
because this love is limited to heterosexuality,
a love rooted firmly in the gender binary,
the kind of love where you save sex for marriage

and don't forget, that part is compulsory.

So pardon my language,
but you can french kiss my ass
if you think love can get wrapped up as neatly as that,
as though ticking every box will guarantee you a happy ending
even if you don't want it.

Love is a choose your own adventure
and you get to fill in the blanks,
a kind of magical Mad Libs
where anything goes.

I took off my rose-colored glasses,
and it turns out
I've been in love the whole time.

That kind of wanting isn't only weddings and engagement rings.

It's stargazing at midnight with 20 of your closest friends, curled up
in a tenderness so vast no four walls could hold it
it's the soaring feeling you get when you hear an inside joke
made only for you
it's warm lazy days by the beach, the sun melting your heart just as
easily as it melts your ice cream
it's running until you can't breathe and then running some more
because you feel like you're flying
it's snagging extra bags of popcorn
from the specialty shop dumpster down the road
because everything's so fucking expensive
but this day-old popcorn is free
and this kind of love is free
and it's *everywhere*, and it's everything, and it's every*one*
and most especially
it is you.

May you wear it like a badge of honor;
may you give it generously everywhere you go.

And may you remember that it is always, *always*
beating through your veins
filling your lungs with air
giving you the courage to say:

"*I* am love,"

and to know deep in your bones
that that will never change.

- hb

I used to think I didn't choose to love,
that love chose me,
I didn't have a say.

According to my mother
it's always been this way.

It should be easy, lemon squeezy
and if it's not
end it, and go get sleazy.
Back then
I was so cold, practically freezing.

But now I think we choose love.

Not the way we choose a show on Netflix
but the way you choose to go back to college even though it's hard
and you're not that good at it.
And aren't you kind of old to be in college?
And what a waste of money.
Even your professors think you know nothing, honey.

Unconcerning.
It's so rewarding knowing you're learning
you're a more informed, spring 2020 issue
your edges untorn, now with 20/20 vision.
This, you choose to do for you, boo.

Love is so rewarding.
But she only blooms when you bathe her in the sun, pour water
down her roots,

and whisper sweet nothings in her leaves.

Care for her deeply, expect nothing in return.

Choose love when everything's a dream.
Choose love when life's in ruins.
Choose love when it's been a long day and your flight's
been delayed.
Choose love when you don't agree and why can't they see things
your way?

Just choose love.

But choose love when they choose love back.
And if for some reason they lack love,
pack your bags and find the love that loves you back.
Life's too short to let them hold you back
and that's a fact.

Now I hope I've made some impact;
it's not what I learned from all my loves
but just from the one that chose love back.

- sl

Fire and Ice
we're not so alike
in dire need of priorities
we fit like a broken puzzle piece
like we weren't meant to be
but some kid jammed us into place.

Nothing about us makes sense.

You drive a Toyota Tacoma
spit out chewing tobacco
into a plastic water bottle

I'm more of a Dodge girl
well manicured, heated seats
drive fast on weathered streets

you eat steak and green beans
I enjoy Asian cuisine
I've tried on every mask in this reality
you've stayed the same:
flannels and dirty denim jeans
when you're upset you shoot rounds
when I'm upset I run around towns

but there was a day way back
when I was panicked to death
I had left my inhaler somewhere unseen.
You pulled my bottom lip down
took a pinch of Copenhagen wintergreen
placed it in front of my teeth

and told me to breathe.

Ever since then I've known.
Known that we were meant to be—
friends in this human sea
and I know you agree
nobody else can see
our watercolor history

as the paint runs dry
my heart stays dyed
all the colored shades
of you and I.

so, Fire and Ice
I think we work quite nice.

- sl

(After April Fleck)

This is real love
grit your teeth love
scrape your knee and jump back to your feet love
don't give a shit love
beat you once in a race and never get over it love.

I'd move mountains for you, babe,
run up and down one and pull it behind me
fight hell and high water for you
catch a hundred spiders, gift them to you
in a box tied up with caution tape.
Because of you, I throw caution to the wind -
I don't know if I've ever thanked you for that.

One rainy day in April
we run in two different heats of the mile
and hit the same splits every lap.
Hearts beating as one
tied together with shoelaces
lungs gasping
running ragged
the ghost of the other at their side
feet bouncing off the pavement like tennis balls -
steady, persistent, and bright.

That? That's real love
fly across the country love
glow-in-the-dark love
reckless and rule-breaking love

a love so deep it aches
I feel it in my lungs when I breathe
when my legs cramp and my feet swell up
I laugh, and I cry
and I'm so grateful
because to feel something that hard is such a gift.
I don't know if I ever thanked you for that either
but I think about it every day.

I run not because I love it,
but because I get to run with you.

I dream about being together, forever
running on an endless sidewalk
in a world where injuries and jobs and geography don't exist
just you, and me
side by side
our shoes scuffing the sidewalk.

Neither of us would know where we were headed
but it wouldn't matter.
We'd run and run and run
go somewhere far
somewhere new
we'd be gone but not lost
because we had each other.

Because we have each other.

- hb

Hope blooms quietly
amid snow in mid-winter.
This is what resilience looks like.

Fear dies softly
at the height of spring's awakening.
Change isn't only for the fall.

Confidence is planted
under summer's heavy rains.
We will harvest it year-round.

A new life is grown
as colorful as the leaves in autumn.
It fears not the bitter cold coming.

This is what living looks like
not bound to one season,
ever growing, ever changing.

To you, dear reader,
we reach out our gloved hand,
offer a small smile,
and hand you a shovel.

This is how you change your life.
This is how the garden grows.
This is what love looks like.

- hb & sl

AUTHOR BIOS:

Hannah Bevis is an asexual and queer writer who first started writing poetry as a middle schooler. She initially fell in love with seeing her name in print when she won the local paper's coloring contest. She loves to read and write, as well as hang out with friends, watch cooking reality shows, and run. She currently lives in western Massachusetts, where she works as a sports writer. *Just Be* is her first book. You can follow Hannah on Instagram at hannah.bevis or on Twitter at Hannah_Bevis1

Photo by Kevin Gutting

Storm Lover is a pan-demisexual poet, author/fiction writer, barber, and owner of a gender-free cutting parlor, The Jade Rabbit. She loves running, observing insects, and writing poems about her exes. She grew up in Illinois and lives in Charlotte, NC. This is her first book. You can follow Storm on Instagram at storm.a.lover

Photo by Storm Lover

VISIT THE PUBLISHER

 **8TH & ATLAS PUBLISHING**

www.8thandatlaspublishing.com

Instagram: @8thandatlaspublishing

Facebook: @8thandatlaspublishing

YouTube: 8th & Atlas Publishing

Twitter: @8thandatlas

TikTok: @8thandatlaspublishing

CPSIA information can be obtained
at www.ICGtesting.com
Printed in the USA
LVHW102013260422
717237LV00008B/843